Margaret M. [signature]

RED
WORLD
GREEN
WORLD

Also by Margaret Chaney

Cracking the Code of Planet Earth

Drone of a Crone (verse)

Red World

Green World

the hidden polarities of nature

by

Margaret K. Chaney

VP

VERITAS

Published by Veritas Publishing
SR 2, Box 817
Sedona, Arizona, 86336

Illustration copyright © 1996 by Drake Design

Cover and book design, editing and type
by **Bard Press**
11505 E. Southern Dr.
Cornville, AZ 86325
(520) 634-4075

LCCN: 96-061118
ISBN: 0-9643261-4-0

Manufactured in the United States of America
by Griffin Printing

thanks

*To my son Don, who helped keep my life
in order.*

*To my son Jack, who helped get my book
in order.*

*To the thousands of strangers still wondering
why they let that fast-talking woman persuade
them to hold out an arm while she showed
them some object.*

*To dear, long-suffering friends who persevere
in speaking to me despite my relentless pursuit
of a vision.*

*To my husband, Bud, who, because he had the
pattern opposite mine, allowed us to crack the
code of planet Earth. And for his love and support,
here and from beyond.*

*And to the Creator and Sustainer of this and all
worlds, who fashioned this design for our use
and left it in plain sight so we could discover it
when we needed it.*

contents

8 Red World/Green World

foreword

As the founder and director of the largest free-standing mental health clinic in New York, with 2000 outpatients and approximately 1000 intakes per year, I had extensive experience with the psychological and physical effects of dietary variation.

Our own research division diagnosed patients on biochemical bases which were not contemporary orthodox medicine, but proved extremely accurate and therapeutic, even with many 'hopeless' patients. Out of this research came the book *Orthomolecular Psychiatry,* (W.H. Freeman, 1973) co-authored with Nobelist Linus Pauling. I was privileged to be elected President of the Academy of Orthomolecular Psychiatry.

At our first meeting, held at Dean's Yard, Westminster Abbey, 130 distinguished clinicians, researchers, and Nobelists arrived from around the world. I remain a member of the editorial board of the *Journal of Orthomolecular Psychiatry,* and was honored to write the foreword to *Cerebral Allergy* by the pioneer in the field, Dr. Marshall Mendell.

My clinical experience made it clear that dietary conditions (such as hypoglycemia) can induce virtually any psychiatric or emotional condition, including grand mal seizures. During electroencephalograms on our ten-channel EEG machine we watched severe cerebral dysrhythmias develop as our nurses placed dilute solutions of various foodstuffs under patients' tongues and recorded changes in clinical condition. The results were startling. Some patients became acutely catatonic in response to certain foods. One 'intractable' patient was subject to violent paranoia triggered by potatoes.

My point is that diet has a great deal to do with how we feel and behave.

I, too, learned basic kinesiology from Dr. John Diamond, and, like Ms. Chaney, used it as a tool of discovery (as reported in *Power vs. Force*, Veritas, 1995). Ms. Chaney has made an important clinical discovery with the potential for enhancing all of our lives. I am pleased, therefore, to be asked to write introductory material to this most useful book.

Accepted medical science is almost always twenty years behind the discoveries of clinicians. The work of Canadian physicians in the '60s demonstrated that natural vitamin E will prevent cardiac arrest—a fact just 'discovered' and announced by the medical establishment in 1996. Many years ago I wrote several articles regarding my twenty-year study of 63,000 patients, which demonstrated that megavitamins could prevent tardive dyskinesia. Finally, this has been confirmed in medical journals.

Ms. Chaney's clinical astuteness is corroborated by my 45 years of clinical and research experience with many thousands of patients. Perhaps in twenty or thirty years the academics will 'discover' her findings—at which time you may be assured there will be no mention of Chaney's work, for she is on what the establishment considers the lowest rung of the academic ladder, a mere layperson, despite her obvious acuity and fifteen years of devoted and scrupulous research.

Chaney's book is innovative, important, and clinically verifiable—the crucial test. I intend to bring her research to the attention of the *Journal of Orthomolecular Medicine* so that my colleagues and their patients can benefit from her dedicated work.

David R. Hawkins, M.D., Ph.D.
Director,
Institute for Advanced Theoretical Research
Sedona, Arizona

preface

My husband was in the hospital; tests were being run to determine if it were possible to coax more mileage from a worn heart. Between visiting hours, I often went home to an empty house and took phone calls from loving family and friends. Other times I wandered in shopping centers, preferring to be surrounded by strangers, who would not ask questions I could not answer.

My greatest comfort was always found in bookstores. There was one book I passed over a time or two but finally bought. It was *BK Behavioral Kinesiology* by John Diamond, M.D., later published in paperback as *Your Body Doesn't Lie*. Dr. Diamond had utilized some of the new research on muscle-function feedback and discovered that our bodies could subconsciously warn us of inimical situations. He had developed a method of analyzing this response. I followed Dr. Diamond's procedures and experimented with his method. It worked, and I became absolutely fascinated, trying it with everyone I could persuade. It was exciting to find we have a readily available diagnostic system inborn, because so much current information about health, energy, and lifestyle is conflicting or comes through suspiciously self-serving commercial channels.

Eventually my husband had successful open-heart surgery. When he came home, I was eager to test the foods we ate to develop the healthiest diet possible.

The results of the muscle-function tests were very clear. Each food either enhanced our strength dramatically, or was immediately debilitating. But, paradoxically, those that made him strong made me weak and those that strengthened me immediately evoked a negative, weakening response from him.

I at first thought perhaps men and women required opposite diets, so I tested many—by now, thousands—of other men and women and found that gender had nothing to do with it. Our world is divided into different basic types of people in some totally unsuspected and unexplained way.

I entered a new phase of my life with a healthy husband, the engrossing study of muscle testing, sometimes referred to as 'kinesiology,' and the strange feeling I had stumbled onto something extraordinarily big.

16 Red World/Green World

introduction

Some time ago, a highly prestigious doctor, involved in some of the early kinesiology work, read of demonstrations wherein muscle-testing of an absent item was done by having the subject merely hold the item in mind—implying that thought itself can adequately serve as a substitute for the physical presence of the object being tested.

The good doctor balked at the suggestion that one's body could react to a substance that was untouched or even seen. But one day while sweeping his garage, he gained a new respect for our subconscious powers of perception. Leaves had blown into a pile in a corner of the garage. He reached to gather them and the hairs on his arm stood up. He pulled his arm back quickly, then cautiously reached in again. Once more the hairs stood up. He stepped back to examine the leaf pile from a different angle. Buried in the leaves was a mother raccoon with a new litter of young. Without the subconscious warning of his body, his arm would have been mangled badly.

The information our bodies transmit is quite literal.

Vibrations are being radiated by all substances at all times. My most dramatic experience of this came as I was testing trees. I walked over to test a silver birch. About three feet from the tree, I was stopped by some kind of invisible barrier. It was as if there were a wall of compressed air barring me. That birch tree didn't want me any closer.

Our muscles in particular have an innate ability to appraise the positive or negative significance of any environmental change. Muscles make the moves that carry us out of trouble; it is only reasonable to presume they receive information as to whether we are safe or imperiled. I used to think the fight-or-flight response was activated once every two or three weeks when a stranger overtook me on a sidewalk or a car in the next lane blew a tire. Now I know that our bodies make an evaluation every time there is a change in our environment—constantly, day and night. Some of these changes might be benign, while others may range from mildly discomforting to life-threatening. Each time we encounter friendly or unfriendly people, noxious fumes, loud noises, food tainted or too hot or cold, chaotic traffic, toxic dyes in our clothing, even glare in our eyes, our muscles prepare for fight, flight, roll-over-and-play-dead, or business as usual.

Throughout the ages, our ancestors relied on subtle mechanisms for intuiting danger in time to avoid it. Muscle-function testing helps us regain that sensitivity which we have allowed to atrophy.

Many biological signal systems work on our behalf, monitoring our internal and external conditions. There are primary and secondary systems. The primary system that warns us of distress may be inscrutable to us, but we can tap into secondary systems to detect these messages. One manifestation of these secondary systems is the phenomenon of muscle-function change.

Usually our bodies size up the situation and take the appropriate action without routing the information through our conscious minds. We reflexively shiver, sneeze, blink, throw up, or say, "No, thank you." Muscle-function testing enables us to eavesdrop on tacit signals from mind to body; we can intercept those messages and observe how they work to protect us.

If you are having physical, mental, emotional, or social troubles, do some investigating. See whether you are trying to eat the foods, use the cosmetics, or take the drugs that nourish and help another category of people but can sabotage your part of the planet's population.

As you grow familiar with the tremendous benefits of this form of self-knowledge, it is only natural that you will wish to pass on the information to others, as I am attempting to do through this book.

A gentle and friendly way to introduce a person to kinesiology is to test with two opposite items at once. Muscle-test first to be sure you are both centered and ready. Then have the subject hold a positive and negative item at the same time; everyone should test weak. Then test with the same items, but one at a time; one should test strong and the other weak. This way the patterns are obvious and easy to understand, and suspicion is allayed that 'You pushed harder.'

As you practice the testing and become familiar with the reactions of people to environmental substances, take notes. Nothing I can tell you will be as exciting or as convincing as the gasp people give when their determination to resist your downward pressure on their arm melts like butter in the sun, or as amazing as the power you feel in their arms as strength is mustered from their mobilized energy.

Your notes will act as a lens, allowing you to see the world in a whole new way.

author's note

In order to talk about different types of people and things, we need labels. We do not want to use 'A' or 'B' because that implies a precedence of one category over the other; '1' and '2' pose the same problem. Someone suggested that what might be involved here is 'fast' and 'slow' oxidization of the citric-acid cycle. If this concept does prove useful in describing diverse digestive processes, it still does not address the issue of opposite muscle responses to such things as trees and rocks, which we'll talk about later in the book. The bio-patterns seem to be linked to electro-magnetic polarities, so 'positive' and 'negative' might well be accurate labels, but in common usage these terms also carry a judgmental connotation that is not appropriate.

Finally I chose REDLIST and GREENLIST as being value-free designations. Even though the RED list contains many red items such as red meat, tomatoes, and some red-skinned fruits, the GREEN list also includes many red items such as strawberries, red raspberries, and watermelon. The colors in the names, therefore, have no final significance beyond giving us labels to easily identify which items show up in which group.

one

polarities of planet earth

If I were to tell you I knew how you could look and feel better, think more clearly, have more sustained energy, and do it all with ease and comfort, you would probably think I was a TV salesperson. But it *is* possible, and there are no requirements of you except awareness and attention. The environment around you is interpretable through a secret code and I am going to give you the key to that code.

There are polar differences wherever we look; some are obvious, some extremely subtle. Human beings have a polarity of male and female in order to exchange energy and perpetuate the species. Now we find that planet Earth operates the same way. All environmental substances appear to be polarized into two diverse groups. We humans do not escape this disjunction; each of us seems at conception to be earmarked for one or the other of these poles, just as if *we* were environmental substances! And as far as the planet is concerned, that is exactly what we are; the planet uses us for its own purposes.

Consequently, there is for each of us a benign part of the environment where we as individuals are sound and a part where, though others do, we do not thrive. This is why so much medical and nutritional advice is contradictory; advice meant for all is accurate for only some and inappropriate for the rest.

We are two strains of people, not one, and there are two precise and opposite groups of foods and other natural or man-made items suitable for each type. These groups look innocently similar, *but don't be fooled.* One group will nourish your body and let it operate at full strength; the other will quietly drain away your energy one bite or one contact at a time.

As you eat foods, drink liquids, take medication, or work in the garden, you gradually notice that some substances make you feel good and others really bother you. You can go along on a trial-and-error basis or you can learn a new way to know in advance which substances match your body type and which are a mismatch.

The test is a simple muscle-function test, often referred to as 'kinesiology.' Many people have used this test to tease out random information about the world without realizing there is an underlying pattern—precise, predictable, and immutable. My test subjects have included over 7000 people including fifty-three sets of identical twins and, through a surrogate, six skeletons (who otherwise had little to say).

There are comprehensive lists in the middle of the book that will show how precise the division is between the two worlds. It might surprise you that the people around you will either echo your type or be antithetical. Each of you will test strong with one list and weak with the other. In spite of all the wonderful things about those other people, if you don't belong in their world, you can't eat their foods without paying a price in loss of energy ranging from simple fatigue to serious physical symptoms.

Later, you can personalize these lists by testing substances unique to your home or profession or lifestyle and adding them to the more than 500 items that have already been tested. Tests with over 7000 people generated these lists; now they are yours to benefit from.

Each time your environment changes, your body assesses your situation. You are constantly tasting a different food, touching another plant or chemical, seeing another person or animal, breathing a new fragrance or pollutant, sipping a liquid, applying a cosmetic or lotion. Some are safe for you as an individual and some are not. You need to know which are which.

As with many discoveries, learning the new is easy; forgetting the old is difficult. But in this case you have at your disposal a reliable test instrument—your body's own muscle system. And the test instrument is deeply invested in your welfare. Ask your body when it feels safe and when it feels threatened. If you ask in the right way, it will gratefully and honestly tell you. The test is easy to learn and is fully described in the next chapter.

There is no long series of questions and answers to memorize; after you test a few items from each list, a technique will permanently establish itself. Our planet obviously functions from a hidden design. I'm sure you have recently seen a high-tech movie. You become totally engrossed with the realism of the special effects. You duck as something on the screen flies toward you and you grip your seat when the action becomes dangerous.

Planet Earth, too, creates an optical illusion. We see a rich tapestry composed of people and things in endless variety. But in truth, everything in our environment is divided into discrete groups and these groups are superimposed, just like the components of the special effects in a movie. The key to cracking the code of planet Earth lies in seeing beyond the illusion and taking a clear look at the workings of the separate worlds.

I have labeled the items in the planet's groups as REDLIST and GREENLIST. Each person then falls into one of four categories: REDLIST male, REDLIST female, GREENLIST male, or GREEN-LIST female. We are accustomed to the difficulties of adjusting to the male and female polarity, but adjusting to these newly discovered polarities of the planet is a more challenging experience.

When a change in the environment is felt to be a threat to you, your muscles prepare for fight or flight. Between the time the potential threat is recognized and the time your muscles take action, there is an instant of limpness as one system disengages and another is activated. This is similar to the moment when the clutch of a manual-transmission car is depressed and the drive train disengages before changing gears.

In that neutral moment, a person doing muscle-function testing can identify your body's response to a perceived threat because you cannot then resist pressure on the selected muscle. (The deltoid muscle across the upper arm is usually preferred for the test because it is both strong and convenient, but any muscle could be used.) If you have ever had stage fright, you may have felt this effect in your shaking knees; as you started to write an important exam, your hand may have trembled; during a job interview, you might have experienced an unpredictable tremor in your voice. Your conscious mind could be full of brave intentions but your muscle system has gone on alert 'just in case.'

Finding that we live with others in an 'oil and water' world does not create monumental problems; the monumental problems already exist! Knowing about them gives us an opportunity to grasp their dimensions and devise some survival strategies. The route to high energy is to identify what energy you already have, bolster it with food and other items suiting your type from the tested list, and avoid substances that belong to the opposite world.

Follow the directions in the next chapter and start testing your reactions and those of your family and friends. You will then be prepared to apply that skill to align your body with its sources of health and energy.

32 Red World/Green World

two

muscle-function testing

Eventually, I took formal training in muscle-function testing, but originally I learned by following the instructions in Dr. Diamond's *Your Body Doesn't Lie*. I was able to recognize quickly what constitutes a valid response. After a few experiences with a compatible partner, you too will realize that you are tapping into an extremely powerful guidance system evolved from primeval times.

Some people who do kinesiological testing take elaborate precautions to ensure that their data are pure. Some insist one hold the sample substance under the tongue so the trilingual nerve will carry information directly to the brain. Some require you to chew the sample, swallow it, and let it start to digest. Others would have subjects rinse their mouths with distilled water between tests, and some ask them to wear only white cotton clothing and remove all metal jewelry. I was pleased to hear in the office of one of the leading kinesiologists that the sublingual test is no longer considered the most legitimate benchmark. Often the patient is now tested while holding the test substance in a bottle.

(It seems unbelievable that we can test substances while they are in sealed containers. If the container is glass, our optic nerves might 'see' what is in it; but our system also picks up the essential vibrations of the test object, and our muscles interpret these signals.)

I recognize there are advantages to rigid standards in any research project. Working under controlled laboratory conditions makes it easier to share and compare data. However, these body signals convey so much energy that they allow great leeway. I believe the over-scrupulous testers referred to underestimate the subtlety, complexity and speed of our biocomputers, operating continuously day and night, checking every change in our environment. Long before a substance disappears behind our teeth, our bodies have made an evaluation of its potential for benefit or harm.

Personally, I do my testing with people actually holding, touching, tasting, or smelling the item being tested. Often they do not have conscious opinions about the items; either they have not looked at them or the items are indistinct (such as pebbles from a handful of gravel). The body nevertheless picks up the information it needs and signals the muscle responce.

On a day-to-day basis, my portable test equipment is either my engagement ring or little salt and pepper packets. I ask subjects to look at and rub the gold and diamond, or hold the salt and pepper packs, one at a time. Testing strong with the gold or salt is REDLIST; strong with the diamond or pepper is GREENLIST. REDLIST nickels and GREENLIST pennies are also handy test tools.

I believe learning to interpret the information sent by our muscles should be an easy, fun process. It involves you and at least one other person: one to test and the other to be tested. Testing takes practice, so plan to do many tests to build ease and confidence. The subtlety and accuracy of the test will come as a surprise to you. Bodies can evaluate signals the conscious mind hasn't even noticed.

This is how to perform the test:

1 Both people stand, facing each other.

2 A strong muscle is used for the test; the deltoid muscle across the upper arm is the most convenient. Thus, the person being tested holds either arm (usually the stronger one) out to the side, slightly higher than shoulder level. As you face the testee, lay your fingertips across his or her arm on the wristbone or slightly above. Place your other hand on the opposite shoulder for balance.

3 Avoid smiling and eye contact.

4 Ask your partner to resist, then apply slow, continuous pressure to the wrist. If the subject's subconscious feels safe, the shoulder joint will lock and prevent your pushing the arm down. However, if it feels threatened, the same amount of pressure allows you to easily push the arm down toward the thigh.

5 To verify that these responses are valid, try this demonstration: first, tell the subject you will smile, then do the test; this should elicit a positive response. Second, inform him or her that you are about to glare and test again. Make menacing gestures as you test, and the subject's response will almost certainly be negative. Even though the person's conscious mind knows you would do no harm, the body warns, "Don't be too sure!"

6 After you and your partner become comfortable with the stance and the test, introduce new substances. Have the person being tested touch something, hold it, smell it, rub it, or even possibly taste it. Anything and everything can be tested. To demonstrate a strong response, let the subject hold or rub an unleaded glass, or hold or smell a lemon. Holding or rubbing plastic, holding or tasting sugar (not sugar substitutes; we'll address those later), or staring at a fluorescent light should be followed by a weak response.

7 As you test items that cause the subject's arm to weaken, the response may be greeted by skepticism. Do one more positive test, pushing much harder than usual to show how strong resistance can be. People differ in their degree of comfort when they find their bodies behaving involuntarily. Some are instantly fascinated. Others fluff it off with remarks like, "It's all in my mind" or "You pushed harder." Most often, though, people realize something remarkable is happening and want to see where it will lead.

8 Let me call strong attention to one quirk in the testing. I call it 'the time-out effect.' The test phenomenon operates for a limited time for each item tested; the response will fade in a few seconds. The system then times out and goes back on alert for the next change in the environment. If you get a negative reaction, the same test after a few moments of contact may give a positive reaction. This does not mean the item tested is no longer inimical; it means the subconscious perception has filed its negative report and moved on. The body is saying, "You have been warned." If this warning is later followed by a rash, headache, or upset stomach, it shows that other systems are still responding to the substance, though the subconscious is now disregarding it.

9 You need to be somewhat cautious about doing too many tests at once. Trade

back and forth, testing each other. Our muscles were designed with endurance capacity
for working in groups, but when we isolate
one muscle to work alone, it soon becomes
tired—and sore! Some kinesiologists aggra-
vate this by applying very strong pressure,
which is not necessary. The signals are so
precise and so subtle that they can be activated with a light touch.

10 By this point you will be able to determine biotypes. You are REDLIST if you
test strong for gold, nickel (~~5¢ coins~~), salt,
or any of the items on the RED lists in
chapter four below. You are GREENLIST if
you test strong to silver, copper (~~pennies~~),
pepper, or any of the items on the GREEN
lists. Most kinesiologists believe they must
test each person with each item but this
information is not random; there is an instant, easily determinable configuration.

11 Infants, autistic children, comatose
patients—those difficult to test—can have
their biotype determined indirectly through
a third party, thus:

a Select a person other than the subject and determine whether that party is REDLIST or GREENLIST.

b Let that person touch the subject. While the testee has contact with the subject, quickly test his or her response. If the test is strong, the subject is the same nature as the patient. If he or she tests weak, the subject is the opposite type.

c If you are skeptical, confirm the results by repeating the test with a person of the opposite nature.

Once we know the patient's biotype, we can be confident the items listed in this book will produce the predicted positive or negative response. Substances not on the lists can be tested by a surrogate of the same profile as the patient.

Testing this way, through a third party, we established that a friend's autistic teenage granddaughter was GREENLIST; then we examined the GREEN food lists. Suddenly the family began reminding each other of moments of alertness the girl had experienced after eating GREENLIST meals and episodes of belligerence following REDLIST meals. It is most unfortunate they did not have this information earlier in the girl's life.

At some point you will inevitably wonder whether it is possible to test yourself. The answer is yes. After all, whose guidance system is it? These reactions are given to us as personal survival tools; no other party's assistance should be necessary.

The key to quickly acquiring self-testing skills is to take advantage of your awareness of the binary nature of this bipolar system. Select some items for testing from both the lists in this book. Have yourself tested to conclusively determine some substances that are positive for you and some that are negative. Then practice. Pick up one of the positive items and pay close attention to any sensations indicating strength. If it is helpful, imagine someone pressing down on your outstretched arm. Then pick up a negative item and be sensitive to feelings of weakness. This alarm system is geared to our basic survival. It reverberates through the whole body and is felt by different people in different ways.

With practice and attention you can take any material—leaves or pebbles or foods—and know immediately to which domain it belongs. One boy says it feels as though a magnet were drawing his blood up during a positive response and down during a negative one. My own signal is a feeling of strength or weakness as I raise my arm and pretend someone is trying to push it down.

I go through grocery and drug stores self-testing, my arm flapping, touching and testing foods and cleaning supplies, vitamins, patent medicines and cosmetics. (My sons spread out their arms and do an imitation of a low-flying airplane, warning, "Here she comes around again!")

I suggest you spend quite a bit of time on two-person testing before you switch entirely to the self-test. You first need objective experience to verify the unique information coming from the tests. And you need someone else involved to give you confidence that the highly visible and dramatic results are not just figments of your imagination. The more skilled you become at the two-person test, the more you will trust the information from the self-test, the messages hidden in the secret code of planet Earth.

three

polarity discoveries

I began testing foods. As my husband came through the kitchen, I held out my arm and asked him to test me while I picked up a food, tasted it, or smelled it. When he pushed on my wrist with slow, continuous downward pressure, my deltoid muscle either contracted strongly enough to lock my shoulder joint, or it did not; my arm either remained parallel to the floor, or collapsed uncontrollably. The results were clearly positive or negative. Then, before he could escape, I asked to test him with the same item. The tests were equally clear-cut with him—just as clear-cut, but with reverse results.

If an item were a 'yes' for me, for him it was a 'no', and if 'no' for me, then 'yes' for him. It wasn't that some, or even many, of the items were opposite; with the exception of less than a dozen, *all* the foods we tested affected us in contrary ways. I didn't have to be super smart to recognize something signicant was happening! I tested other men and women and found the patterns gender-neutral. I checked young people, old people, blood relatives, racial groups, ethnic groups. I corralled friends and strangers to check and re-check the same things. If anyone was strong with green beans, as I was, they were also strong with pork, cauliflower, oatmeal, sour cream, and orange juice. If they were strong with watermelon, as my husband was, they paralleled his proclivity for haddock, rice, and skimmed milk. In each case, everyone went weak with the items on the list opposite theirs.

I kept notes and made more lists. If one item on my list tested the same with someone else as it had with me, every one of their items corresponded to mine. If one item tested as on my husband's list, all items tested did. There is an old adage: if you want to know whether all crows are black, you do not have to see every crow; you just have to find one white one. In testing well over 7000 subjects, I have found no white crows.

What had seemed at first random data rapidly took shape as a distinct code. In the quiet, mysterious way that developing film transmutes from blank paper to a face smiling up at you, there appeared two separate lists of foods. The items on the two lists formed a binary split—discrete, distinct, and mutually exclusive—an obvious and elegant polarity.

I was not prepared for this finding. One pattern with so many variations as to be virtually patternless, I could have expected. Or there might have been twenty or thirty major patterns with significant differences. But just two? That had extraordinary implications.

I began to wonder—what if all foods in the world fell into two separate groups? It would logically follow that we should eat from the group matching our polarity and avoid the other. Our closest family members and best friends might be able to share our foods—but maybe not; maybe they would need to eat from the other group. Foods from one group might nourish us while foods from the other group might irritate us.

Allergic reaction is, essentially, the body's rejection of a substance because it is to some extent an irritant. In that sense, we might be nourished by half the food in the world and find the other half pathogenic. An allergist might say, "Poor you; you are allergic to six or eight substances." But this new theory implied that, to differing degrees, you are allergic to thousands of substances and are fortunate that only six or eight are giving you serious trouble at this time!

The overwhelming evidence I accumulated compelled me to believe this improbable hypothesis to be fact. I tested each food time after time with many diverse people, and found that even when our bodies display a tolerance that lets us eat a food from the opposing list with no obvious adverse effect, our muscles still warn us of its unwholesome quality for us. That evaluation never changes. The only possible conclusion is that we are two kinds of people living in two interwoven but distinct environments.

We do not readily recognize that the environment is composed of two strands because the strands are so large and tightly intertwined and the filaments are so small and innocent-looking. We have the same problem an ant would have separating human beings into the two bundles we know as male and female from the evidence of only an eyelash, drop of blood, or toenail. We are accustomed to seeing the environment whole, never dreaming of a disjunction between half its components that totally isolates them from the other half. What clue could we have that oranges, oak trees, rubies, vanilla, and one half of the population have a unique relationship with each other, a relationship in complete opposition to boxer dogs, sterling silver, nutmeg, and the rest of the populace?

As the two lists grew longer, I thought I had exhausted most of the useful information available from testing foodstuffs. Then one day, with a disturbing curiosity, I remembered my spice rack. What if spices were not just innocent, flavor-enhancing substances? What if they also played their part in this strange dichotomy? As I tested them, they clearly disclosed that each belonged to one list or the other, and none to both. For example, the REDLIST includes allspice, cinnamon, thyme, sage, vanilla, salt, bay leaves, oregano, and paprika; the GREENLIST includes cloves, nutmeg, dill, garlic, pepper, marjoram, and mint.

While I was telling a GREENLIST friend about my findings, she noticed my scented candle was vanilla and asked if we could please blow it out. Within ten minutes, her bleary eyes, runny nose, and dull headache (all of which had started after she entered my house) completely disappeared. The same thing happened on another occasion with two other GREENLIST guests. Nowadays, unless all my guests are of the same list, I use lemon-scented candles (lemon being one of the very few foods that show up on both lists).

When I have talked to people about the two food groups, many have dismissed the information, saying, "I can eat everything." There is a deceptive apparent truth in this assertion. We do seem to have a considerable level of tolerance for many items to which our bodies react negatively when tested. That makes it tempting to think there is a large group of neutral foods common to both lists. In fact there are only about a dozen which test strong with both categories of people. These include lemon, vitamin A, vitamin C, mushrooms, spirulina (a fresh water algae), coffee (except for the chemically processed brands), honey, fructose, and some (not all) poultry and eggs.

What people probably are actually saying when they claim they pay no attention to what they eat is that their subconscious systems are steering them to the right foods. However, if the guidance system is an inborn biological survival device, shouldn't it be working perfectly for everyone? Maybe it once did, but is now thrown askew by the modern proliferation of food additive and drug technologies. It is possible that long ago, REDLIST people broke off a sassafras twig to chew, while GREENLIST people nibbled on cattail roots. At one time GREENLIST people might have spent the winter longing for the first sun-ripened strawberries and REDLIST folk might have fantasized biting into a new tree-ripe apple. Today, with modern supermarkets offering every food in every climate in every season, we seem to have scuttled our natural guidance system.

Actually, people who claim they can eat everything usually do not. As I watch them eat, I see they tend to reject many foods on their opposing list. They justify their choices with excuses such as, "Skimmed milk tastes like chalk," "Whole milk tastes greasy," "Bananas back up on me," "I don't care for white fish, but I love shellfish," or "Why do they always put parsley on my plate?"

Hopefully, having read this far, you will not be prey to such illusion. Even though you have no reason to be suspicious of a certain food, testing will definitively indicate whether your body will respond negatively to foods that might not be listed here but are not native to your biotype.

People who assert they can eat anything often ignore evidence of physical degeneration as if there were no connection between their nutrition and such things as poor complexion, low energy, chronic disease, and strained personal relationships. Also, they often ignore signs of discomfort from others who are eating from the menu the 'eat everything' person has prepared. Parents who brag about not catering to a child's finicky appetite would be appalled to learn that the child is just trying to survive, suffering from a diet of incompatible foods.

Unfortunately, our culture puts obstacles in the paths of our natural tastes. Children eating with parents of the opposite pattern will be told, "Drink your orange juice," "Finish your oatmeal," "Eat your carrots," "Liver is good for you." Each of these admonitions is correct for one half of the population, but potentially troublesome for the other half.

To have eggs and poultry appear on both lists came as a real surprise. The original testing showed eggs and poultry, except for the livers, to be GREEN-LIST. REDLIST tested fine for egg whites but not egg yolks or poultry. I thought there might be a problem with the lecithin content of the yolks because both as a diet supplement and as a baking-pan spray, lecithin registers 'no' for REDLIST. Then a doctor demonstrated to my sister-in-law that his organically raised flock of poultry and their eggs were fine for everyone. We realized that the problem had to be with the feed.

I went to the poultry nutrition department of a state university and tested feed additives—the vitamins, antibiotics, and hormones used to control growth and prevent disease in large commercial flocks. The tests indicated a clear REDLIST/GREENLIST split. The additives that tested 'no' for GREENLIST are neutralized by the digestive chemistry of the poultry and end up being acceptable to everyone, but the 'no' additives for REDLIST are still 'no' throughout the whole cycle.

I checked the poultry and eggs in six supermarket chains. All were proper for GREENLIST but only one-third passed the test for REDLIST. It is possible for REDLIST people to find suitable commercially marketed poultry and eggs, but it requires constant alertness to variations in the product due to changes in poultry feed. The expensive way to check is to buy the eggs and test them in the privacy of your home. The realistic way is to put your hand on the carton in the store and have a friend test you then and there. Better yet, alert the management in charge of purchasing and request that only poultry products safe for all of us come to market.

Vitamin A and vitamin C supplements can be either REDLIST or GREENLIST depending on their source. If one happens to test 'no' for you, a change of brand could rectify that. All the other vitamin and mineral supplements are on one list or the other, not on both. We are told that our bodies require nutritional supplements from outside sources; that advice needs to be reformulated in two different versions.

When I tested spirulina and found it to be on both lists, I was very excited; it is the first universal almost-complete food. Both soy and rice have strong advocates who proclaim each to be the one basic food. Neither meets my criteria. Soy products, in-

cluding tofu, infant formulas, and all the soy deriva-
tives, feed REDLIST people nicely; rice is strong for
GREENLISTs. But they do not cross over. The entire
cultures that apparently thrive on one or the other
supplement their diets with local fruits, vegetables,
fish, and small game.

Spirulina, a fresh-water algae with a green-
grass color and odor, is sold in health food stores as
a soft, floaty powder, or capsules, or pressed into
tablets. It can be stirred into water and drunk quickly
to provide total nourishment, lacking only fiber and
fat. Added to fruit juices, it enhances their fresh
flavor. As an ingredient in familiar recipes, it in-
creases nutritive value impressively. Spirulina registers strong with both REDLISTs and GREENLISTs.
It is a first-level product of the sun's energy. Energy
in such primal form can apparently nourish us all,
but as it travels farther up the food chain through
plants and animals, the split takes place.

Whole coffee beans processed without chemicals in a simple, natural manner test safe for everyone. Even those caffeine-based products sold as
stay-awake aids will usually register 'yes' for both
groups. However, coffee with additives or constantly

changing chemical supplementation, as well as coffee processed by acid baths, flaking, or some types of decaffeination must be checked out brand by brand.

Although tests show coffee and caffeine to be universally acceptable, this flies in the face of the personal experience of many people and is contradictory to several scientific studies. It may be that by producing a surge of glycogen and insulin, caffeine induces attendant biochemical changes that would be of value in a fight-or-flight situation. In that case, the body would read coffee as valuable for survival purposes; our continuous indulgence for non-survival purposes may accumulatively become unhealthy.

Coffee drinking tends to be done in two styles. REDLIST people enjoy it and drink it, sometimes moderately and sometimes in great quantities. GREEN-LIST people are more apt to taper off coffee looking for substitutes, or discontinue drinking it altogether. If they then seek out teas or herbs in its place, they must test each beverage separately. None of the teas tests neutral; some varieties are REDLIST and some are GREENLIST.

The battle rages on about honey. Natural food enthusiasts make extravagant claims for its properties, but many nutritionists say calories are calories and many dentists say sweets are sweets. My findings show that both body types accept honey, but both reject even the most minute quantity of refined sugar, white or brown.

Classic experiments with children demonstrate that they will help themselves to foods in a seemingly erratic fashion, with excesses and omissions, but will eventually balance their selection naturally over a period of time—unless sugar is available. Sugar subverts the natural subconscious food-selection process in just a few days. If it can do that so quickly, imagine what it has done in a couple of generations when consumed at the massive rate that has become our national habit. Kinesiological testing dramatically demonstrates the dimensions of the problem. Place a few grains of sugar in the palm of someone's hand or on their tongue and do the test; down goes the arm!

Fructose, a form of natural sugar that does not produce an insulin reaction, finds acceptance from both body types. Saccharin tests have been confusing. I have samples of effervescent saccharin that test 'yes' for everyone and samples of standard tablets which are 'no' for everyone.

One of the most popular sugar substitutes surprised me. I intended to demonstrate to some friends that it was incompatible to both body types. Instead, both groups reacted favorably. I repeated my tests back home with some of the product left from previous tests; the older product still tested 'no.' It seems that without fanfare the manufacturers altered the product in a way that made it more biologically acceptable. I hope future 'improvements' do not reverse this change.

If you start testing foods and other substances with your family and friends, keeping notes on the results, you'll soon be ready to match your lists to mine. It is unlikely that anyone will test safe to sugar, chocolate, many processed foods, or some of the mixed vitamin combinations. A few foods may show up on both lists along with cotton, oxygen, silicon, potassium, and a small wildflower of the mint family, *prunella vulgaris* (known, interestingly, as 'heal-all'). I have done extensive testing of local and imported foods and products. So far, the items indicated are the only ones I have found common to both lists; all others fall into either one sphere or the other. Generally speaking, people and foods always diverge into two domains.

Thus I reasoned it was possible that the whole environment is similarly split. Soon I was testing creatures, trees, plants, rocks, crystals, body-types, liquors, the periodic table, patterns of male baldness, mother's milk, magnetic fields, mental states, fossils, 150-year-old skulls, diseases, relationships, and the metabolisms of identical twins.

Each of these experiments had a story and a lesson. Each story was different, but the lesson was always the same: all environmental substances fall into two kingdoms; each of us is created to live a happy, healthy life in one realm, but not in both. We are at risk when we venture into foreign territory. When we mix the two kinds of food, we interfere with the delivery of fuel to the brain. This leads to fatigue, depression, anxiety, confusion, and even tearfulness. Then come allergies in all shapes and forms.

Recognize and avoid those things that drain your energy. Often adjusting just one or two items can relieve a chronic malaise. Study the lists that follow and keep testing new items as you come across them. Identify and classify your own environment as quickly as possible and start to reap the benefits.

four
the lists

Please be aware of what these lists are and what they are not:

They are
- the result of scores of tests with these items.
- limited—they will change as more tests are done.
- an invitation to experiment, discover and learn.

They are not
- a panacea for all your ills, problems, and distress.
- laboratory tests in any of the biological disciplines.
- the final word on anything—that is for future studies.
- a proposal that you radically change your diet; they only offer suggestions for gradual modification.

I make no recommendation that you adhere exclusively to either list. Each person has his or her own level of individual tolerances. Before you commit to adopting any of the items on these lists, test them yourself and form your own conclusions.

The lists are an analysis of over 500 items including meat, fish, dairy products, fruit, vegetables, grains, nuts, seeds, spices, herbs, teas, fats, oils, liquors, trees and plants, creatures, jewels, metals, leathers, furs, fibers, chemicals—ultimately, whatever I could get my hands on.

Over the course of testing, the lists have been constantly updated as anomalies appeared, usually due to over-quick generalizations about categories.

As soon as I can identify varieties I will include them on updated lists; but you can't wait for me. Learn the testing. Start working on your own lists.

The ultimate list would be a carefully controlled appraisal of every item on the planet. And each of these substances and each of these creatures would attest over and over that the code of planet Earth says, "*Look again; there are two worlds.*"

meat, fish, dairy

REDLIST	GREENLIST
beef	buttermilk
butter	**cheese**
cheese	cheddar
braided	colby
cottage	farmer's
cream	feta
kash kaval	Gouda
Monterey jack	mozzarella
Tilsit	Muenster
clams	Parmesan
cream	provolone
eggs (some)	pot cheese, dry
fish	ricotta
monkfish	Romano
salmon	Swiss
sardines	eggs
shark	**fish**
tuna	cod
frog legs	haddock
gelatin, unflavored	herring
lamb	orange roughy
liver	perch
lobster	snapper
milk, whole	turbot
pork	whitefish
oysters	milk (skim, 2%)
poultry	poultry (not livers)
shrimp	yogurt (skim milk)
tofu, other soy	
yogurt (whole milk)	

fruits, vegetables
REDLIST

apples
  Red Delicious
  Macintosh
  Jonathon
  Granny Smith
asparagus
avocado
beans, all kinds
blackberries
blueberries
bok choy
broccoli
Brussels sprouts
cabbage
cantaloupe
carrots (some)
cauliflower
celery
chard, Swiss
cherries
  red
  black
chives
collards
corn
cranberries
cucumbers
escarole
figs
  Kadota
  Mission
  Calimyrna
grapefruit
grapes, red & black
leeks
lemons

lettuce
  Bibb
  Boston
  romaine
mushrooms
mustard greens
napa cabbage
olives, black
onions
  red
  bermuda
oranges (most)
papaya
peas
peppers
  bell
  green
  red
plums
  purple
  red
potatoes
  sweet
  white skin
pumpkin
radishes, red
raisins (dark)
rhubarb
scallions
spinach
squash, spaghetti
sugar cane
tomatoes (most)
turnips and greens
watercress
watermelon, yellow

fruits, vegetables

GREENLIST

apples
  Golden Delicious
  Cortland
  Ida Red
  Red Rome
apricots
bananas
beets and greens
carrots (some)
cherries, Queen Anne
coconuts
coriander
currants
dates
eggplant
endive, red endive
figs, Greek
gourds
grapes, green
kiwi fruit
lemons
lettuce
  iceberg
  leaf
mangoes
mushrooms
nectarines
okra

olives, green
onions, yellow
parsley
peaches
pears
peas
  Canadian yellow
  split yellow
  split green
peppers
  hot
  pimento
potatoes, red skin
radishes, white
raisins (light)
raspberries
squash
  acorn
  crookneck
  Hubbard
  yellow
  zucchini
strawberries
tomatoes
  Italian plum
  yellow
watermelon, red

spices, herbs, teas

REDLIST	GREENLIST
allspice	aloe vera
artemisia	anise
Sweet Annie	black cohosh
Silver King	blessed thistle
Silver Mound	carob
basil	catnip
chervil	cayenne
cinnamon	chamomile
coffee (some)	cloves
comfrey	coffee (some)
cornstarch	cumin
cream of tartar	dill
dong quai	fructose
fructose	garlic
gelatin, unflavored	honey
golden seal	lemon verbena
honey	marjoram
horsetail	mei yen
jojoba	mint
maple syrup	molasses, dark
meat tenderizer	monosodium glutamate
molasses, dark	nutmeg
spirulina	pepper
tapioca	rose hips
tea (some)	spirulina
thyme	tea (some)
turmeric	vinegar (white wine)
vanilla	
vinegar (red wine)	

grains, nuts, seeds

REDLIST	**GREENLIST**
alfalfa	barley
almonds	bread (rye or barley)
buckwheat	brazil nuts
caraway seeds	cashew nuts
chia seeds	coffee
corn	flax
coffee	fenugreek seeds
fennel seed	macadamia nuts
millet	pecans
oats	pumpkin seeds
peanuts	rice, rice flour
pistachio nuts	rye
poppyseed	sesame seeds
soy	walnuts, black
sunflower seeds	
triticale	
walnuts, English	
wild rice	
wheat	

fats and oils

REDLIST	GREENLIST
butter	chicken fat
corn oil	coconut oil
cottonseed oil	lecithin
safflower oil	olive oil
soy oil	sesame oil
sunflower oil	
vegetable short- ening	

liquors

bourbon	beer
brandy, black- berry	**brandy** apricot
corn likker	raspberry
gin	champagne
grenadine syrup	creme de menthe
kirsch	rum
tequila	sake
vermouth,dry	Scotch
vodka	vermouth, sweet
wine (red—dry to medium)	whiskey
wine, white	wine sweet heavy red
Bianco	Concord

Niagara	**wine** (most white)
	  chablis
	  sauterne

jewels, metals, miscellaneous

REDLIST	*GREENLIST*
amber	agate
amethyst	coral
jade	diamond
opal	emerald
ruby	garnet
sapphire	jasper
tiger eye	pearl
turquoise	topaz
quartz	brass
aluminum	bronze
antimony	copper
gold, white gold	lead
platinum	silver
steel	tin

fabrics

cotton	cotton
nylon	linen
wool	nylon
	silk

critters

ant	butterfly
crab	cankerworm, fall
crayfish	caterpillar
grasshoppers	cockroach
housefly	coral
lobster	cricket
millipede	jellyfish
praying mantis	octopus
scorpion	snail
seahorse	tarantula
snake	weevil, white pine
sponge	
starfish	
spider	
toad	

trees and plants
REDLIST

amaryllis
ash, Arizona
baby's breath
beech
cactus, Christmas
camellia
cedar
cherry, weeping
chicory
chrysanthemum
clover, sweet white
columbine
cyclamen
elm
euonymous
fern, staghorn
forget-me-not
geranium
goldenrod
grass
  Kentucky blue
  Marion blue
  monkey
heal-all
hibiscus
holly
huckleberry
hyacinth
Indian paintbrush
ivy, English
jade plant
jasmine
juniper
laurel

lilac
lilies
lupine
magnolia
mahogany
mahonia
mandrake
maple
  sugar
  Japanese
milkweed
mimosa
mullein
myrtle, crepe
oak
palm
philodendron
pigweed
pine, white
pittosporum
primrose
Queen Anne's lace
redwood
roses (some)
Solomon's seal
spider plant
spruce, blue
sumac, staghorn
teak
thistle, Russian
tulip
violet
walnut, English
willow

trees and plants
GREENLIST

aloe vera
bamboo
birch
  silver
  river
  paper
boxwood
cactus (some)
carnation
cattail
chestnut, horse
coleus
cypress
elder, box
ficus
grass
  red fescue
  rye
hackberry
heal-all
hens and chickens
hydrangea
maple, silver
mint
moss, air

nandina
oleander
olive, sweet
orchid
pachysandra
pine
  Norway
  Norfolk Island
plantain
poinsettia
poplar
redbud
roses (many)
rubber plant
sorrel
thistle
  bull
  sow
vetch
walnut, black
wax plant
yew
yucca

five

polarities of body and spirit

Now comes the fun part—shortcuts.

It is a rule of nature that all creatures' bodies adapt to their food supplies. What better way to eat ants than to have a snout like an anteater? A giraffe is elegantly designed for browsing tender leaves from the tops of young trees. If REDLIST and GREEN-LIST food supplies are different, should not our bodies be different? Absolutely.

Our diets are so similar that we have erroneously assumed they were interchangeable. Our bodies are equally similar. But although the differences are not great, differences there are indeed. REDLIST and GREENLIST bodies vary in eye motion, cranial balance, shoulder shape, knee structure, thigh-muscle formation, and patterns of male baldness.

Let us start with obvious examples. Look for an elegant posture with a ramrod straight spine, and the back of the neck flat between the shoulders and head; you will be observing a typical GREENLIST body.

GREENLIST shoulders are straight across; arms hang straight, clearing the torso. A really extreme GREENLIST physique looks as if the hanger is still in the jacket.

At rest, a GREENLIST chin lies against the neck or chest. When a GREENLIST has been holding still, the next move of the head is a pivot to the right or left as if on a surveying tripod, the top of the head holding level. Sometimes the head remains still while the body rotates. The chin lifts straight up and down. If the top of the head tips in any direction, it moves as a unit with the body, sometimes down to the waist or even the toes.

GREENLIST eyes are wide open. When looking around, the glance shifts abruptly from object to object while the head holds still. If a GREENLIST person develops poor posture, the back will 'break' below the shoulder blades and fall forward. The chin will then not hug the neck or chest, but will still maintain its other characteristics.

REDLIST people are most easily described by their contrast to GREENLISTs. REDLIST heads move around in an animated manner, especially during conversation. The back of the neck is curved between body and head. The first motion of the head after holding still will be a change of axis from both the vertical and horizontal plane. With poor posture, the shoulders slump forward and the chin and nose rock upward.

REDLIST eyes are not totally open, especially the bottom eyelids. REDLIST eyes focus on an object, then wander to the next object, wander again, and refocus, the head following simultaneously.

REDLIST shoulders slope away from the neck. Arms curve around the sides of the chest. Part of this bearing could come from heavier trapezius muscles across the shoulders, but its genesis is primarily in bone formation.

Muscles originate or are attached to the patella in such a way that GREENLISTs have depressions above and below their kneecaps. If the party is thin, this creates a 'knobby knee' appearance. REDLISTs have a depression below the knee but quadriceps muscle mass covers the top of the kneecap.

GREENLIST thighs are cylindrical, maintaining almost the same dimension from knee to torso. The gracilis muscle on the inner thigh lies flat and creates a space between the thighs just above the knee. The posterior hamstring muscles are long and tendinous, creating the appearance of a break with the gluteus maximus. GREENLIST people always have a handful of empty cloth under the seat of their slacks, but they can wear narrow trouser styles with an elegance REDLIST people envy.

REDLIST thighs are cone-shaped. Even slender, well-exercised thighs slope outward from knee to torso. The top inch is a dead give-away, wearing out blue jeans, squeaking corduroys, and bulging the sides, to the delight and enrichment of exercise salons around the world, who promise to make these protrusions disappear. (They never do!) On the outer thigh, the heavier muscles keep skirts and slacks from hanging straight, as required by high fashion, but on hard benches they pad us while our GREENLIST friends squirm.

People make the contradictory observations that GREENLIST thighs are slender and REDLIST thighs are muscular—both because they are well-exercised. However, a glance around any athletic training camp will demonstrate that athletes in top physical condition still display the two distinctive thigh formations.

As we will elaborate in our discussion of relationships, we usually team up romantically or professionally with someone of the opposite body-type, as a glance at couples' physical characteristics will confirm. Watch ice dancers, for instance. If the woman's thighs are cylindrical, her partner's are usually conical. Yet both bodies get the same workout and both move with the same grace and power.

In two classic patterns of male baldness, the high forehead is GREENLIST and the bare circle at the crown is REDLIST. Oriental lore holds that the bald crown is caused by eating too much red meat and the bald front results from eating too much fruit.

My observation is that regardless how men might eat, food compatibilities are determined by one's REDLIST or GREENLIST disposition.

Muscle-function tests show that 'identical' twins tend, in fact, to be bookends—reversed pairs, one of each type. A check of their body formations confirms this. We are so busy pointing out ways identical twins are alike physically and psychically that we ignore the evidence that they do not live in the same world metabolically. A study done at the Monell Chemical Senses Center at the University of Pennsylvania revealed that identical twins eat far from identically. The researchers surmised that the twins were just trying to be different from each other, but in a double-blind study, the subjects would not even know each other's choices. Identical twins eat differently as a matter of biochemistry, not whim.

Our two body designs are equal in almost every endeavor. The Olympics illustrate that neither REDLISTs nor GREENLISTs dominate particular sports. Only one sport—running—seems to favor GREENLISTs. If you observe the two types walking together, you will notice a certain GREENLIST advantage in grace; this becomes more pronounced at a run, as the legs move differently in their hip-sockets. It is most often a REDLIST youth who hears from his track coach the disheartening words, "You aren't built to be a runner." Similarly, most football quarterbacks are GREENLIST, but all the other positions are filled by both REDLISTs and GREENLISTs.

Your first reaction to these generalizations might be to point out exceptions in details that you've found in your friends or self. Try working from a broader base. Test a group of people and give each person a red or green marker. Then ask them to gather in two separate groups and look them over carefully. You will be impressed. They will appear as different as two separate species. And once you see it, you can never stop seeing it.

We have all heard that

> *Jack Spratt could eat no fat,*
> *His wife could eat no lean*
> *And so, betwixt them both, you see*
> *They licked the platter clean.*

This is one of the few references I find in literature to the two biotypes. And it is usually distorted by illustrations depicting the couple as caricatures of an emaciated Jack and roly-poly wife. This is not suggested by the verse. In spite of bodily differences, our natural eating patterns do not normally lead to such distortions.

Once you recognize the two patterns visually, you can practice gathering data while people-watching. I enjoy seeing whether the contents of grocery carts in checkout lines identify REDLIST or GREENLIST shoppers. One day an obviously REDLIST woman leaned across my cart to look at a bin of avocados and asked of no one in particular, "I wonder whether I can eat those." I surprised her by saying, "Yes, you can, but stay away from those green grapes and that iceberg lettuce."

Muscle tests are the easiest and most accurate indicators of the two types, but after a period of practice in matching tests to body shapes, the body shape alone will suggest an accurate identification. A more subtle indicator yet is temperament. REDLIST people tend to be more animated; GREENLIST, more composed.

Were five men talking together in a group of whom four were GREENLIST and one REDLIST, the GREENLISTs would appear beautifully poised, like statuesque reeds undulating in a gentle breeze. The REDLIST fellow, by contrast, would seem like an animated character darting around in a video game. Were the proportions reversed, four REDLIST men would look like high-energy leaders trying to animate a GREENLIST zombie. After some observation, the distinction is readily recognized.

In narrow aisles of stores, REDLISTs bend and weave to accommodate passersby; GREENLISTs hold their ground. Unbidden, REDLISTs often give way to GREENLISTs because they see that they 'cannot be swayed' and interpret this as a position of earned power. GREENLISTs, in turn, watch REDLISTs' dynamism and constant intensity with some anxiety, often responding by trying to control or subdue this natural REDLIST energy. It's a wonder relations between the two kinds do not turn to complete mayhem!

Along with the folk saying, "Opposites attract," should go another: "Opposites intimidate!" As you read over the attributes of the two patterns, think back to times you despaired because you could not attain the qualities of the other profile. Studies show 90% of women to be unhappy with their bodies; I think we are intimidated by the opposite conformation.

When we compare ourselves to someone of our own ilk, we forgive our shortcomings. We say he or she is younger or has more free time to exercise or has more money to spend on clothes. But when we compare ourselves with someone of the opposite pattern, we come unglued! We sign up for exercise classes, buy diet books, mumble, and make stupid remarks.

Think carefully about what is happening. If people of the opposite nature intimidate you, you likely intimidate them. Check out the differences and enjoy them. "If you've got it, flaunt it!" As I counted, all but ten models in a seven-hundred-page fashion magazine were GREENLIST. I was consoled by the fact that the cover girl was REDLIST.

Once you can identify the dancers, watch the ballet woven as two sets of people move in and out of each other's worlds. Play, and learn how exciting the watching game is. The discovery of a new polarity is a new key to life's mysteries; dash around to see what locks it will fit!

The most interesting area of inquiry is learning about relationships. There are, again, two different kinds: the *dynamic* relationship between a REDLIST and a GREENLIST, and the *supportive* relationship between two people of the same mold.

As we examine differences in lifestyles, we usually find we have paired up dynamically, with a partner of the opposite kind. My testing, so far, indicates that in twosome relationships—marriages, friendships, business partnerships, or ice dancing teams—five out of six couples are mixed REDLIST and GREENLIST. Thus, only one couple in six are matched in biotype.

'Opposites attract' comes to mind again. That saying has traditionally been applied to extreme opposites and attended by bewildered head-shaking. We wonder how, in light of such impediments, couples could still choose to attempt going the same route. Actually, in milder form it happens all the time. And frequently the differences create a nice balance.

It may be that we look at another person, instinctively recognize qualities we lack, and know at some deep level those qualities could provide the security of complement and equilibrium. Or, on the darker side, perhaps we see a worthy adversary with whom to contend—to sharpen our strengths or satisfy a need for conflict. Or, as part of the survival design of the species, we might subconsciously seek a mate who would not compete for the same foods. I doubt we'll ever know.

It is not uncommon when a new corporation is being formed for each person invited into the planning and executive process by a GREENLIST leader to be REDLIST, confirming the effectiveness of working relationships between people of opposite natures. On the other hand, sometimes we come together with our peers in a common interest, looking for support rather than dynamic exchange.

What relationship we seek when we select our pets is another question of interest. Since they come into our lives, often unbidden, in such a variety of ways and wiggle into our hearts regardless of their origin, I wondered how we would choose if we went about it intentionally. The local dog show gave me the opportunity to check, as breeders make considered choices. I was able to test twelve breeders and surrogate-test their dogs. In all twelve pairs the breeder and dog were the same type. Apparently, given a choice, we would pick a pet who reinforces our strengths and provides a supportive relationship instead of the dynamic interaction more common among human pairs.

As I watch relationship choices, I am absolutely astonished by two insights: what a lovely, smooth life it is for couples who are the same type—and how seldom that happens! There may be fewer couples of the same pattern because it seems like looking in a mirror. A pair both of the same list must beware of narcissism on the one hand and monotony on the other.

People with opposite characteristics energize each other. The dynamics of mixed relationships stimulate personal growth. But at some point an alien ambiance can cease to be an energy source and become an irritant, mentally, physically, emotionally, and socially. I am disturbed at the price sometimes extracted from individuals negotiating such relationships, feeling their way with so few clues to go by.

In spite of what else about mixing disposi-
tions might have great potential, we should not be
obliged to eat each other's food. We must honor our
chemical differences and search out our proper fuel
if we are to function at full capacity. The wrong fuel
in a car can be destructive. As automobiles have
distinctive fuel-tank necks for different gas types, we
should be born equipped with differently designed
mouths that would allow us to eat only REDLIST or
GREENLIST foods!

People living alone or eating with a matched
partner probably will not even recognize what I am
talking about; the subject simply does not crop up
as a problem in their lives. Since their chemical fuel
supply is good for both partners, their health and
energy level are fine and calmly regular. Families with
matched biotypes drift into natural food selections
and appear to escape many of the crises of daily life
that beset the rest of us.

There seem to be numerous advantages to
relationships where the parties are matched. Living
in a dietary relationship with someone of the same
pattern reinforces the natural selection process. These
couples develop a rhythm in their lives from shared

metabolic styles. They both want to stop for a snack after a movie, or they both want to go straight home; they both prefer to sleep late and skip breakfast, or to be on the tennis court at dawn. They display a lifestyle resembling the unison behavior of a school of fish, and aptly fit the description, "They get along swimmingly."

When our relationship choices lock us into a partnership with the opposite biotype, we are forced to regularly negotiate, compromise, and manipulate. This goes on so consistently that many mixed couples think it's the only way to live. And perhaps it *is* that dynamic that keeps the folkways and mores stirred up and fresh. Maybe the five couples, struggling away, make the world go 'round, while the matched pair of the sixth couple simply smile and get a free ride.

88 Red World/Green World

six

dietary polarities

Shortly after you begin listening to your intuitive wisdom regarding specific foods and start making your first menu adjustments, you may very well collide with the realization you are living in a dietary relationship with someone whose nutritional needs are exactly the opposite of yours. How do you compromise?

You don't.

Look back over your medical and vital history; how much more of that do you want? Check your present physical and energy levels; contemplate a future when your reserves will be further depleted.

When we disrupt our natural metabolic processes, we interfere with glucose breakdown and the energy supply to the brain. This collapse leaves us vulnerable to fatigue, depression, confusion, and anxiety, accompanied or followed by more severe physical manifestations.

If you have been eating alone, you might be in tune with your natural selective process, to your advantage. Nearly everyone has irrational likes and dislikes for certain foods. This is a natural sign to let us know our needs. What if these preferences are not random but predetermined by our categories?

REDLIST people can contemplate a diet of GREENLIST foods and know it would leave them hungry for something more satisfying—a buffering of fat, more complex carbohydrates, more 'gut wadding.' GREENLIST people, aware of their bodies' problems processing fats, recoil from REDLIST foods as 'greasy.' They would rather recombine elements of their shorter food lists, sometimes even repelled by food unless it strikes their fancy at the moment.

REDLIST and GREENLIST attitudes toward food depend on who's assigning the labels. REDLISTs consider their appetites to be robust; GREENLISTs call them 'piggy'. GREENLISTs see themselves as discriminating; REDLISTs think they're 'picky'. Of leftovers, REDLISTs gleefully say, "Oh, there's some more of that good stuff"; GREENLISTs shudder, "No, not again!" As REDLIST folk study the GREEN food lists, they are dubious anyone could subsist on such skimpy rations; GREENLIST people read the RED lists and make slight gagging sounds. Our bodies have their own wisdom.

In the past, women stayed home and did the cooking. Many of them would admit to denying their own food preferences and adjusting menus to suit the likes and dislikes of other family members. After all, who wants to cook what others will greet with a "Yuk!"? Over a period of time this self-denial takes its toll, first in mental distress and then in physical breakdown. But the Victorian stereotype of women as helpless and confused has finally been banished. Women are out of the house now, freely eating their choice of lunches and often dinners. No longer does the convention persist that women are a habitually neurotic species. The passport to liberation may be not only a job, but also a personally selected diet!

Look at the RED list and the GREEN list right now and recall whether the foods of the one assortment have made you feel better than the other. Ask yourself if you have been eating in accord with someone else's taste. Look over your list carefully and imagine a private diet composed thereof.

I have spent many hours checking the cookbooks of organizations committed to health. Cookbooks are available from groups concerned with weight control, heart disease, diabetes, cancer, allergies, and hyperactive children, in addition to macrobiotic and vegetarian cookbooks and the miscellaneous data available from nutritional science and the USDA. All recognize a distinct link between nutrition and the manifestation of physical malaise.

With a RED or GREEN pencil, I mark the separate ingredients in each recipe or recommended food list. So far, these specialized cookbooks defeat their own purposes. REDLIST and GREENLIST foods show up together in nearly every recipe. Often it would be possible to make simple substitutions of ingredients and still maintain the essence of the meal, but this requires some circumspection. When I, REDLIST, fell asleep in my chair after a meal of

GREENLIST chicken chop suey and GREENLIST rice, my daughter-in-law threatened, "Next time I'll serve you REDLIST pork chop suey on REDLIST oatmeal!" Ugh!

The real world intermingles people of each classification. We are commonly born into families with mixed biotypes, and usually marry someone of the opposite mode. Such situations require our full creativity in the day-to-day problems of food preparation. Here are some suggestions; you surely will think of others.

1 Go through your cookbooks with RED and GREEN pencils, marking each ingredient in each recipe with the appropriate color. It is possible to adapt recipes and substitute ingredients to get the format you require.

2 When shopping, buy matched REDLIST and GREENLIST items: whole and skimmed milk; Romaine and iceberg lettuce; almonds and pecans; beef and white fish. Menu selection is easier if the ingredients are on hand.

3 Store the foods in separate areas. It is helpful to see your options at a glance. Stack the REDLIST bean soup and tuna fish on one end of the shelf and the GREENLIST split-pea soup and canned beets on the other end. Keep REDLIST oranges and celery in one refrigerator bin and GREENLIST peaches and zucchini in another one.

4 Set out a RED bowl and a GREEN one, each containing appropriate snacks for each type.

5 Unless you switch to two wholly separate menus, you will probably continue to make familiar dishes that rely more on ingredients from one list than the other. I suggest you cook enough to have leftovers. The next meal can feature a recipe favoring the opposite list. The third meal can then be comprised of separate servings from the leftovers.

6 A meal with the main dish from one list can be supplemented with several side dishes from the other list. Don't try to conform to your partner's dietary preferences!

7 Take full advantage of kitchen technology, cooking and freezing individual portions, then microwaving them at mealtimes.

8 Or, as my five-year old son said when we were trying to stretch our holiday dinner candles until Christmas Eve, "We could eat out more often!"

I sympathize with people who would like to attempt the REDLIST/GREENLIST menu plan but find it too confusing. One friend says that until foods come in RED and GREEN packages, she'll never be able to remember which is which. Group menu decisions are usually made by one person, and adjusted slightly to cater to individual likes and dislikes. Even cooking a medically prescribed diet necessitates only a few substitutions to regular family menus. But adherence to the REDLIST/GREENLIST system requires far more than simple adjustments, as it involves two mutually exclusive sets of ingredients.

Such food planning is all in a day's work for a trained dietitian, who could take a given set of ingredients and design attractive menus, recipes, shopping lists, and cookbooks as well as color-coded cafeterias and packaging. (Carry this book with you when marketing and keep it handy in the kitchen. Or use the enclosed form or write to the address at the end of chapter ten to order a handy, purse-size laminated RED/GREEN shopping and menu guide).

This system of analysis could be of great value in structured dietary regimens. Let's look, for instance, at the usual foods on the athlete's training table, arranged in a REDLIST/GREENLIST chart.

food	red	green
steak	✔	
spaghetti	✔	
red tomatoes	✔	
parmesan cheese		✔
bread	✔	
butter	✔	
whole milk	✔	
skimmed milk		✔
orange juice	✔	

If all athletes were REDLIST, this diet might work, but pity the poor GREENLIST star! One of my cousins was a GREENLIST basketball player who fell into a slump. I advised him to try a cheese omelet, head-lettuce salad, and skimmed milk before his next game. His parents (unbiased!) reported he had never played better or with more clever strategy.

In the corporate executive dining room it is stylish to order white wine, broiled white fish, and rice pilaf. My advice to the REDLIST gang is, sneak out for a bowl of chili and crackers before you get so sleepy you give away the store!

Business personnel may have the largest food budgets and the most immediate material payoff. But the greatest nutritional benefits would come from home kitchens, two separate lines in school cafeterias, and adjusted menu selections in hospitals.

In schools that have a one-menu lunch, it would be possible to observe the effects as differing needs are or are not met, thus:

1 Test each student for RED or GREEN identity. Use an identifying marker such as a

RED or GREEN piece of yarn to tie on their arm. This is preferable to physically separating them into two groups. We commingle instinctively and can feel stressed in a group of only our own type.

2 Evaluate the lunch as being RED-LIST or GREENLIST.

3 Score late-afternoon behaviors such as math tests, sports skills, or study hall alertness.

Institutional populations are notoriously discontented with their food. Assign people to tables of all REDLIST and all GREENLIST diners, then make a quick check of leftovers. If the GREENLIST tables consistently leave three-quarters of the oatmeal and the REDLIST people hardly touch the beets, much money could be saved by menu adjustments. In addition, morale and the level of physical and mental health would be improved.

In situations where there is only a take-it-or-leave-it menu, I suggest you find a partner of the opposite nature and survive by barter.

The other day I ate in a cafeteria with a REDLIST mother and her GREENLIST daughter who had chosen the same salad. The mother ate her REDLIST ham and left the GREENLIST lettuce, turkey, and Swiss cheese. The daughter poked at the ham but polished off every single bite of lettuce, turkey, and cheese. I enjoyed their creative rationalizations when I pointed out their actions. The mother said the ham was closest on her plate, the turkey tasted funny, they gave her too much lettuce, and she wanted to get to her pie. The daughter insinuated that no one should eat ham, although she neither keeps kosher nor is a vegetarian; she just *knows* no one should eat ham! Had they ordered one salad and two plates, they would saved money and both have been happy.

Menus of fast-food chains could be adjusted easily. For REDLIST patrons, hamburgers with Romaine lettuce on a bread with no yeast or malted barley. For GREENLISTs, chicken dipped in egg and rice flakes, malt barley in the buns, and heavy on the sesame seeds. People seek salad bars and health-food restaurants in an attempt to take nutrition seriously. But just being raw and fresh does not make a dish jump into both lists. Beware generalizations.

Allergy cookbooks, for instance, ban whole families of foods when one member proves to be a problem. But their classifications are often invalid. All apples are grouped in one family, yet Red Delicious apples are REDLIST and Golden Delicious are GREENLIST. REDLIST blue grapes and GREENLIST green ones also defy the single-family concept.

This came to my attention when a friend developed trouble with tomatoes. She was told to avoid all of the nightshades. But I tested the family thus:

food	red	green
deadly nightshade		
most red tomatoes	✔	
italian plum tomatoes		✔
yellow tomatoes		✔
potatoes, brown skin	✔	
potatoes, red skin		✔
eggplant		✔

Denying her this whole family unnecessarily limited her dietary choices and she was deprived of valuable low-cost foods.

Obviously there are similarities and divisions that make groups of foods acceptable or unacceptable to REDLIST or GREENLIST people, but the categories follow obscure biochemical distinctions instead of traditional botanical categories. We must simply recognize that this is yet another example of our planet's innate propensity for polarities. Along with day and night, up and down, male and female, and a multitude of others, the REDLIST/GREENLIST dichotomy applies to all of the environment, including us humans. Fortunately, we have our subconscious to steer us. If you just start experimenting, your body will advise you.

I would like to be able to say something bland and conciliatory like "as long as we're young and healthy, none of this need be taken too seriously." But I cannot. Babies come into the world with their configurations firmly established. If for whatever reason their immune systems are weak, difficulties show up immediately. Problems with infant feeding are legendary. I was four months old when peaches

(GREENLIST) came ripe in our area. If my nursing GREENLIST mother ate a peach, I (REDLIST) broke out in a rash.

The ingredients listed on commercial infant formulas are mostly soy-based. That is fine for RED-LIST babies but not GREENLISTs. Some of the formulas include coconut oil, excellent for GREEN-LIST babies but not for REDLISTs. If a soy formula were to include a different oil or if the coconut oil were added to a different protein base, the combinations would more closely suit the needs of babies, whose modes I find to be established from birth (no doubt from conception).

It is shocking and sad to discover that not even mother's milk is innocently neutral. It mirrors the mother's type! If mother and baby are the same biotype, things are fine—madonna and child. If they differ, several unpleasant things can happen. Should the mother choose foods mostly from her realm, the baby will suffer. If through instinct or advice she happens to eat foods of the baby's type, the child will do fine; but the mother, on a diet that interferes with the glucose supply to her brain, can develop mental difficulties such as fatigue, depression, anxiety, and confusion. We lump these symptoms together as the 'postpartum blues' syndrome and expect her to 'snap out of it!'

At the beach I watched a slender, attractive REDLIST mother with her four-year old GREENLIST son and her year-old REDLIST daughter. Thinking she might enjoy some adult conversation, I wandered over to ask some of my endless questions. She said she had successfully nursed both children; they obviously had strong, lovely bodies, clear skin, and eager attitudes. I asked, since she had successfully nursed her GREENLIST son, had she by chance been put on a nursing diet including skimmed milk, head lettuce, chicken, fish, low salt, etc.? She smiled and said yes. Then I asked about her mental health at that time. Her face clouded over as she remembered the period as being one of unbearable depression. Then I asked if she had cheated on the diet while she nursed the little REDLIST daughter. Her guilty grin made us both laugh.

seven

polarities of daily life

The disjunction of this world into two divisions follows no apparent logic. I have searched for objective criteria, but so far have only kinesiological testing of the muscle system and a visual concept of the structure of the human body to rely on.

For a time I thought apples were on my husband's list and not on mine because the Golden Delicious apples he chose for his lunch were 'yes' for him and 'no' for me. But two days in a row I sent him off with Red Delicious apples. He developed 'I'd-rather-be-dead' cramps; I ate the rest of them and felt fine. That's when we began to notice that my list often included red-skinned apples, red- and purple-skinned grapes, red and purple skinned plums, red-skinned onions, red cherries, red radishes, and red wine. My husband ate the same things—apples, grapes, plums, cherries, radishes, onions—but in their green- or white-skinned versions. However, just when we thought we could use color as a criterion, bright green Granny Smith apples proved to be REDLIST, and gorgeous, shiny Ida Red apples tested GREENLIST.

On realizing they do not do well with beef, pork, and lamb, GREENLIST people often label themselves 'vegetarians.' Actually, they don't thrive on vegetables alone. Except for beets, squash, iceberg lettuce, leaf lettuce, endive, eggplant, okra, yellow onions, and parsley, most veggies are REDLIST. GREENLIST people best accommodate fruits (except for citrus, cantaloupe, and red- and purple-skinned varieties of green- and white-skinned fruits).

Testing sometimes exposes changes from the original designation of a substance, but when an item transfers to the other list, it is no longer found on the first—never straddling both lists. For instance, my carrots had tested as REDLIST. One week two GREENLIST friends called to say they had found their carrots GREENLIST. As we all shop at the same market, I checked the new brand of carrots I'd just bought, and indeed they *were* GREENLIST. Later, in a garden shop, I tested packages of carrot seeds. All of them were REDLIST except Imperator Long.

The memory of the day some friends helped me test whether liquors follow the same binary division always reduces me to giggles! And they certainly do. On the REDLIST are gin, vodka, bourbon, tequila, blackberry brandy, kirsch, most red wines (except heavy, sweet ones), and also one or two brands of beer. On the GREENLIST we find most of the beer, as well as rum, Scotch, whiskey, peach and apricot brandy, crème de menthe, white wines, and champagnes.

Check out someone 'crying in his beer' or 'in the clutches of demon rum' and you may well find a REDLIST person drinking GREENLIST drinks. I am not trying to promote drinking but should we choose to use alcohol, we would do well to be sure we are drinking from our 'yes' list.

I spoke to a weight-control group one evening and asked the audience to use my observations on

I had never consciously connected any of these problems to the food I had just eaten because nothing ever upset my stomach, gave me a headache, or produced any other vestige of typical digestive mischief. We are blessed with very forgiving thresholds of tolerance, so even though you may be RED-LIST, many GREENLIST foods will never give you overt trouble (though others very well might). Examine the food lists and start experimenting for yourself; the payoff can be well worth the trouble.

Friends who start adapting their diets to my lists tell me tales of auspicious results as they learn to acknowledge their natural tastes. One GREENLIST person said, "I couldn't do everything at once, so I started eating Golden Delicious apples instead of Red Delicious ones. All of a sudden I realized I really do not like potatoes; I just like the chicken gravy I put on them." Another GREENLIST friend whose energy had dwindled until she found herself wandering aimlessly from room to room all day, switched from a REDLIST oatmeal breakfast to a GREEN-LIST rice one. Now she is in an assertiveness training group, taking a microwave gourmet cooking class, and back to doing stone sculpture!

posture and divide themselves into two groups on opposite sides of the room. The REDLIST people were mildly angry and frustrated about their weight problems, but the GREENLIST group was sunk in despair! The GREENLIST members felt they had tried everything to reduce their weight; only when they cut their calorie count to a level so low they could barely function could they lose any weight. And the consequent mental depression and physical fatigue extracted a price almost too high to pay.

The members of each group compared their common problems, tastes, lifestyles, and frustrations. By the end of the evening, one person in each group was absolutely certain she was not in her proper group. Nothing said there seemed appropriate to them and everything the opposite group said expressed their exact feelings. I tested these two women, and it was true—their original appraisal had been in error.

Living in the wrong culture for just forty minutes made these people definitely want out! This impressive phenomenon gave everyone in the room some insight into the enormous problems of living with someone who has an opposite biological makeup. I asked everyone to guess the patterns of the family members in their home. Nearly everyone concluded the people they normally ate with were of the opposite biotype. Much of their common weight problem was in fact a mixed-diet problem.

My REDLIST friends have all endured disbelief and scorn from diet counselors when they gained weight on diets based on skimmed milk, lettuce, rice, and white fish. Each of those foods creates a unique reaction in REDLIST people (as do tuna, liver, and cabbage in GREENLISTs) that can sabotage a weight-loss program.

I periodically spend a few days in a social situation that leaves me physically exhausted, mentally confused, and more than a little angry and sad. If this is compounded by extra-hot or extra-cold weather, I find myself totally wiped out! However, if I stop at the local roast-beef restaurant on my way home, ask to have some of the fat left on my meat, choose a baked potato and some green beans, and by-pass the free beets, horseradish and dill pickles, I emerge with a smile on my whole body and am back in the land of the living. As mentioned, I am conspicuously REDLIST. These same choices would leave a

GREENLIST person irritably belligerent, and would probably lead to a restless night.

To my GREENLIST friends, I say, "If you need to be sharp mentally for an important meeting, do not let anyone buy you steak, baked potato, and spinach salad; they will end up with all of your marbles! Make your order white fish, rice, and a head lettuce salad." And I warn my REDLIST friends that if they want to stay awake, they should order just the opposite or simply go hungry.

My husband and I spent years eating and enjoying foods from both lists. However, once I knew we each had a different biotype, I had to wonder what damage we had been doing to ourselves. How much of our disastrous medical history could be attributed to this cross-eating?

Between us we logged high blood pressure, hypoglycemia, miscarriage, vein stripping, obesity, fatigue, and assorted surgeries. We did not smoke, our meals were home-cooked and fresh, and we had been intelligent and moderate in our lifestyles. But, both over sixty and having pushed our tolerances to the limit, our condition could be labeled 'brittle.' Each time we discovered our bodies sending a negative message about a certain food, we dropped it from our personal menus. The results were swift and varied, but always obvious. Each food played out its own little drama.

I found that omitting my habitual one-half scrambled egg at breakfast for just one day eliminated pains in my finger joints. Now I avoid eggs at home, but I occasionally order them in restaurant breakfasts when I meet friends. At some time in the early afternoon after those breakfasts, pain will hit one of my finger joints as if someone had jabbed it with a thumbtack.

By dropping iceberg lettuce for about five weeks, I jettisoned twenty pounds. Eating chicken puts me to sleep for the next three hours. Lecithin in bread gives me ringing in my ears. Malted barley, included in most baked goods, can plunge me into sadness and black depression. A mysterious discoloration down one side of my chin disappeared two days after I discarded a mint-flavored toothpaste. Bread yeast makes me so water-retentive I clump around the house as if in wooden shoes for about 36 hours until the water suddenly lets go!

People get caught in food traps these days because seemingly authoritative advice comes from all directions and fosters guilt for not following *all* of it. For example, the inclination of the bodies of GREENLIST people is to have as little fat as possible in milk; however the message from the bodies of REDLIST people is to use milk in its natural state. But the current nutritional dogma is that *everyone* should switch to skimmed milk.

Salespeople for health-food products tell us alfalfa roots go deep into the earth, bringing up a abundant supply of minerals. But although RED-LISTs test strong to alfalfa, if GREENLIST bodies find it inimical, should GREENLIST people allow sales talk to override their bodies' own messages?

eight

medical polarities

The distinction of people into two metabolic sets has major medical implications. For instance, we definitely should *not* use each other's medications.

I tread lightly here and include the standard disclaimers. I give no medical advice nor should it be taken as such. These observations may sensitize you to symptoms and coincidences you might not have noticed before but they can be professionally evaluated only by a licensed medical practitioner for diagnosis and prescription.

However, the quality of medical care you receive is based on the data you provide, and the concepts introduced in this book could be most helpful in that area, allowing you to work cooperatively with a sympathetic doctor. Beyond that, what you can do in the way of self-treatment and therapy is limited only by your desire and determination.

We are conventionally expected to submit to blood tests, urine analysis, x-rays, and electrocardiograms. These tests are inconvenient at best—expensive, embarrassing, and slow. At worst they involve pain, bruises, collapsed veins, barium distress, excessive radiation, and other risks. Often the system most quickly and easily available to monitor symptoms of malaise is muscle testing. Muscles are as much involved in the full functioning of our bodies as blood, urine, or electrical impulses. Muscles can be trusted to carry valuable information about our present state and do so without discomfort or delay.

Since medicines and combinations of medicines fall into REDLIST and GREENLIST categories, the answer to the riddle of how one person can benefit from a medicine that is devastating to another becomes obvious. Those who should most appreciate this are doctors themselves, whose first pledge is *"Do no harm."* If a doctor took into account a patient's REDLIST or GREENLIST makeup, he or she could adjust prescriptions far more efficiently.

One of the major dangers of our lifestyle is the growing incidence of unhealthy side effects from prescription drugs or combinations thereof. Sometimes the term 'side effects' is just a euphemism for direct effects of the wrong drug. My original suspicions about prescription drugs arose from seeing friends rummage through their purses on social occasions, and come up with bottles of medicine, which they tested. I found it striking that if a drug tested negatively, the patient almost invariably confessed, "I've already stopped taking that one." The human body's acuity is far greater than we commonly recognize.

My testing has included patent medicines, prescription drugs, narcotics, and the synthetic narcotics used for pain control in terminal cancer. Medicines derived from animal, vegetable, or mineral sources can be tested in their original state. If the medicine is in manufactured form, smell it, touch it or taste it, and perform the test. If contact is not advisable, test while holding the bottle or box. You will find that sometimes brand-name products and generic equivalents test alike—and sometimes they don't. If you have developed your skills in self-testing, you can get an instant reading by yourself. If the doctor's office does not maintain samples to test, the pharmacist should be willing to sell you one pill before filling the whole prescription. This will give you preliminary information; you can return to your doctor for advice from there on.

Casual conversations with friends have led me to unexpected avenues of investigation. A member of the medical staff of a terminal-care unit was frustrated and depressed because so many of the drugs available to ease the pain of dying patients produced toxic side effects. Instead of bringing peace and comfort, the drugs increased the agony of many patients. This immediately sounded to me like a REDLIST/GREENLIST dilemma.

I went to the local police station and asked if I could examine some of their confiscated narcotics. They brought out a large case of labeled samples used for teaching and identification. The officer helping me was GREENLIST and I , as you know, am REDLIST. We tested the narcotics and they showed a definite bipolarity.

Then I went to the terminal-care unit. The staff was just finishing lunch, so I drew up a little chart and tested the food on their trays. When they brought out the drugs, we tested those and added them to the chart. The results were a perfect illustration of Earth's polarity.

A nationally prominent specialist in diabetes invited me into his examining rooms to test his patients. Of the first eighteen, sixteen were GREEN-LIST and only two REDLIST. When I pointed this out, he contemplated the fact that his medications and diet advice were all designed for GREENLIST patients. His success with so many GREENLIST patients masked the inappropriate treatment of his rarer RED-LIST patients.

I sometimes work backwards to confirm the validity of my testing. I notice people who are wearing medic-alert tags and find out which drugs give them trouble. Then I check whether they are RED-LIST or GREENLIST. The results have invariably corroborated the theory proposed here.

Orthopedic surgery has accomplished miracles in repairing body mechanics. When replacement is successful, new limbs and joints permit new lives. An ever-present problem, however, is rejection of foreign substances by the body.

A patient was scheduled for hip replacement. Her surgeon taped slivers of the four replacement materials to her forearm. Three samples were inert but the fourth created a red spot. He decided to defer the surgery until he could find an alternative for that substance. My muscle testing paralleled his observations, so I arranged for another orthopedic surgeon to allow me to test the materials *he* uses in prostheses. Of six plastics and metals, two were suitable for either REDLIST or GREENLIST; two were for REDLIST only and two for GREENLIST only. These simple tests provide a quick preliminary way to evaluate new materials coming on the market as technology 'advances.'

A GREENLIST acquaintance had been having repeated knee surgery. The quadriceps muscles on the front of her thigh would not stay attached to the patella. The doctor had high hopes for a suture using umbilical cord, but that was also unsuccessful. If the cord was from a REDLIST fetus, I wonder whether a GREENLIST cord might have held?

One brand of heavy-gauge plastic pouch filled with liquid solution for breast implants is 'no' for both REDLISTs and GREENLISTs. I discovered this when a specialist referred a patient to me for testing because the woman's whole life had deteriorated in the two years since she'd had surgery to enlarge her breasts.

The attempt to manufacture new drugs to suit everybody is bound to miss its mark. There already are excellent REDLIST and GREENLIST medications; what we need is a specific determination as to which is effective for which biotype.

My husband and I both came down with flu and sought medical attention from different doctors; we each came home with an antibiotic and a cough syrup. It was a fortunate coincidence that his medications were GREENLIST and mine were REDLIST. We followed our instructions and recovered quickly. However, had we both gone to the same physician, we would both have received the doctor's same drugs of choice. Had that been the case, one of us might not have had so swift and successful a recovery.

When my husband reacted badly to medication after open-heart surgery, we tested his four prescriptions and identified one as suspicious. His doctor prescribed a substitute and the problem was solved immediately and conclusively.

Marvelous advances have been made in medicine by using careful scientific protocol. I have three suggestions as to how the REDLIST/GREENLIST concept could aid basic research.

1 Divide patients into REDLIST and GREENLIST before dispensing placebos and experimental drugs. Recently there have been two major research projects for heart-attack victims. One study used some traditional REDLIST therapy, the other a new GREENLIST wonder drug. Both studies claimed impressive success. Unfortunately, the statistics, which showied positive results for around 25% of the subjects of each test, obscured the fact that the 75% failure rate included 50% from the opposite body type, who could actually have been harmed by the test. The results would have been truly spectacular if those patients could have been withdrawn from the study in advance, before being exposed to risk.

2 Animals and cultures being used in experiments should be tested for their REDLIST/ GREENLIST constitution, because they too necessarily fall into one of these two groupings. Results cannot be universally valid if innate bias exists in the research.

3 Be aware that certain diseases are predominately REDLIST or GREENLIST. Each group demands its own treatment, no matter how successful another treatment has been for the opposite group.

It is interesting for me to watch the medical field deal with new concepts. Laws originally designed to protect the public from a quack with a new chemistry set or a do-it-yourself home brain-surgery kit now make it difficult for laypersons to interact with licensed professionals. The only role for which I am authorized at present is the compilation of careful notes, whose value will be evident when I am able to share them with impunity.

nine

polarity mysteries

What has most puzzled me from the outset of my discoveries is the question of what exactly is going on here. Knowing that some of us are native to one domain of the planet and some to another would be less disturbing if we could understand this as some part of a clear global design.

I therefore set out to test Earth's environmental materials with as few variables as possible. I began with the elements of the periodic table and found it a bewildering experience. Of twenty-three tested so far, only three—oxygen, silicon, and potassium—are common to both REDLIST and GREENLIST; the others split into the usual dichotomy. Our bodies are composed of many of these elements, which are replaced regularly. The only explanation for two mutually exclusive reactions to the raw materials for this replacement is that they are somehow buffered in combination or transformed in absorption.

I filled in squares of a periodic chart, seeking an orderly arrangement to offer some explanation of our mysterious metabolic polarity, but my entries hop-skipped around with no theme whatsoever.

I tested people with an old horseshoe magnet painted green on one half and red on the other. GREENLIST people were strong when holding the green, or north-seeking pole, and limp holding the red (south-seeking) pole. REDLIST people tested conversely. Not knowing what the magnet might have been through over the years, I bought a new one at a science museum to double-check. The results were the same; REDLIST people are magnetized to south poles and GREENLISTs to north poles.

Then tests with fossils embedded in rock ages past showed a trilobite to be REDLIST and a cephalopod to be GREENLIST.

I even had an opportunity to examine skulls and other bones of remains being moved from a small military cemetery during construction. Through surrogate testing, I determined that the 150-year-old skeletons were still REDLIST and GREENLIST. The biotype was plainly encoded in the bones.

Part of an answer was suggested when I found identical twins to repeatedly be one REDLIST and one GREENLIST. As mentioned above, since everyone concentrates on how much physically and psychically alike identical twins are, they overlook the fact that the twins live in two different metabolic worlds, in spite of having developed from a single egg. Polarity seems intrinsic to our world. Instead of a simple bipolar partition of male and female, if we take into account REDLIST and GREENLIST categories, we humans, as noted, then form a quadripolar model: REDLIST male; REDLIST female; GREENLIST male; GREENLIST female.

There are more mundane oddities, too. GREENLIST includes green olives and olive oil, REDLIST, black olives; yet black olives are pressed to produce olive oil! REDLIST counts pumpkins, but GREENLIST gets pumpkin seeds. REDLIST claims oysters, GREENLIST, pearls. REDLIST owns sugar cane; GREENLIST takes the rum made from it.

If single foods can be baffling, combinations are even more so. It seems that in certain mixtures of foods, separate ingredients neutralize one another sufficiently for everyone to be able to eat them. Culturally, that is the way we have always functioned. We serve REDLIST/GREENLIST mélanges such as macaroni and cheese, lamb and mint jelly, pretzels and beer, fish and chips, strawberries and shortcake.

Then there's lasagna, composed of REDLIST hamburger, REDLIST tomatoes, GREENLIST cheeses, and GREENLIST noodles, thereby registering 'no' for everyone. If we use less meat, more cheese, and substitute Italian plum tomatoes for regular red tomatoes, lasagna remains a 'no' for REDLISTs but now becomes a 'yes' for GREENLISTs. Or if we increase the amount of hamburger, add sausage, switch to cottage cheese and Monterey Jack and retain the standard tomatoes, we can transform the same basic recipe to a REDLIST dish.

This raises the issue of what mechanism operates when foods are combined. Do some combinations simply mask negative signals of their inimical ingredients? Or does a total chemical transformation take place? Frances Moore Lappé, in *Diet for a Small*

Planet, describes how, remarkably, legumes, grains, seeds, and nuts that lack certain essential amino acids necessary to provide whole protein become complete protein when eaten in the right combinations.

Two items on *her* lists that supply each other's missing amino acids are peanuts and rice. But peanuts are REDLIST, rice, GREENLIST. Would the combination then be on both lists? In fact, it turns out to be on neither! First, I tested a mixed handful of dry peanuts and dry rice. When that tested 'no' for both types, I added water, heated the mixture, and put it through a blender. The resultant mush was still a 'no' for both forms. The mixture might have become a *chemical* protein, but apparently not a *biological* one.

REDLIST peanuts, however, mixed with RED-LIST sunflower seeds, become a complete protein for REDLIST people while GREENLIST rice and GREEN-LIST sesame seeds comprise a complete protein for GREENLIST people. Thankfully, our body's sub-conscious detection faculties usually can evaluate combinations as well as separate ingredients.

We have yet to address the role of mind in these two patterns. Psychologists have demonstrated that some people, allergic to flowers, will sneeze around artificial flowers if they believe them to be real. Also, traditional medicine has documented instances of people ingesting known poisons and yet, through the power of rigorously disciplined minds, remaining unharmed. Recent research has shown that convincingly presented placebos can be as much as 60% as effective as the medicine they imitate. In view of the large tolerance we already have for each other's environments, it is not unreasonable to wonder whether a practiced mind could entrain itself to the opposite pattern. Yet people adept in many forms of mind control still go about in bodies that give off typical 'yes' and 'no' signals. Regardless of their metaphysics, their corporeal incarnations register the same REDLIST and GREENLIST indicators as everyone else.

Another supposition arose from the Fur and Jewel list I compiled, initially as a joke for some of my friends. It was just before Christmas and I wanted to help them with their gift 'hinting'. Rubies, amethysts, and sapphires proved to be REDLIST; diamonds, topaz, and emeralds tested GREENLIST. Gradually, I realized that many of the jewels on the lists were crystals. When I think of crystals, I'm reminded of radio frequencies. Could it be our brains are 'wired' with two different kinds of circuits, delivering opposite responses to the environment?

After testing many, many people for food tolerances, I began to be able to predict in advance if they were going to reject something. I could not foretell when they were going to accept, only when they were going to reject. I considered the possibility I could be influencing the result by anticipation, or might be biased in some other way. Since this is a major danger in experimental work, I analyzed the signals accompanying my premonitions.

I began to notice a swoosh of air go over my shoulder as a subject's body rejected the item. Closer observation revealed that the air between us seemed to vibrate during the test. The most precise description of what I felt would be a phenomenon analogous to something hitting me in the chest—like tiny droplets of a sneeze. It was as though the person's biofield stiffened, setting up a shield as something inimical approached, a shield so real I felt it.

A thirteen-year-old boy questioned me about it. I stood about two feet in front of him and told him

I would pick up something negative for me. He became very still, then grinned from ear to ear and said, "It felt like little rays went into me." I demonstrated it for a grown man. I had closed my eyes. As I opened them, I thought it might not have worked because his friends were laughing—at him staggering backward as though he had been pushed in the chest.

I do not know what form this shield takes. It's feasible that it is a permanent envelope of energy that bubbles out intact to ward off danger. But if it is composed of units of energy that surge out to do battle with perceived danger, then dissipate, that is a more disturbing prospect. How many times can we afford to lose our energy as we attempt to deal with an hostile environment? And how much energy could we conserve if we learned to remain more in our own spheres?

I keep searching for historical evidence of some awareness of the two biological families. How could it have remained unnoticed? Yet I have not found even veiled references in Native American legends, Greek or Roman mythology, old writings from the mid-East, Egypt, India, China—nor in any literature from fairy tales of diverse lands to the most contemporary technical anthropological classifications.

Commonly, when I ask if someone knows of any such systematization of human duality, the yin and yang distinction is mentioned. The concept of yin and yang implies a blending in wholeness, primarily between the sexes, but it is much too vague to predict the specific responses of groups of people to particular environmental substances patently disclosed by muscle testing.

What could be the purpose of two kingdoms? Early in my research a friend refused to believe there could be two domains. She said, "God would not do that." We know now, 7000 tests later, that whoever designed the universe (or is it duo-verse?) both *would* and *did* do that.

But why?

I had established to my satisfaction the fact that all foods, vitamins, spices, herbs, medicines, liquors, and narcotics divided into two separate configurations appropriate for two strains of people. I saw two groups of people so different that their skeletons, muscles, and body mechanics were visually identifiable

But I wondered if my context might be too limited. This polarity is not just about people—it's about the planet! As human beings, we already have a most obvious polarity: male and female. A similar polarity exists in the rest of our world, as I became aware when a young friend told me she was to have scratch tests for a possible allergy because she developed distressing symptoms whenever she mowed the lawn. (Who doesn't?) I suggested she go outdoors, bring in some grass and weeds, and we would see what muscle testing revealed. She came back with red fescue grass, yew, cedar, and milkweed. She tested weak to the grass, as suspected, weak to the yew, and strong to the cedar and milkweed.

That was when I first realized that nonfood substances were as bipolar as the foods in the supermarket. I enlisted several people from both lists and tested them. The results disclosed that vegetation fell into REDLIST and GREENLIST divisions as clearly as the tested grocery-store foods.

The following week I vacationed in northern Michigan. As I walked along the back roads and beside the lake, I tested grasses, weeds, wildflowers, trees, shells, rocks, and feathers. Everything fell into one or the other class. Only edible mushrooms occurred on both lists, and only poison ivy and poisonous mushrooms appeared on neither.

Growing together in a square foot of soil were many plants, half of one sort and half the other. A roadside plot of weeds including chicory, Queen Anne's lace, sassafras, milkweed, and dandelion would register strong to REDLISTs and deplete the energy of GREENLIST people. Another small patch might support cattails, sorrel, and mint, energizing GREENLISTs and sapping the strength of REDLISTs. Trees, even after being cut down and made into furniture, can still register their type: REDLIST people respond negatively to birch; GREENLIST folk weaken when they touch oak.

Family members have brought me back things as foreign as a handful of gravel from Finland, inside the Arctic Circle—ten stones. Five were GREENLIST (though only two of these looked alike) and the other five were REDLIST. It is astonishing how the planet can be so consistent in dividing its environmental substances into these two categories.

I came to the realization of what an intimate role the planet plays in the lives of human beings. Some of us are made of the dust of one half and the rest made of the dust of the other half of the two interlocking halves of the planet. The sand from Sleeping Bear dune in Michigan is GREENLIST. The sand in the picnic area of the Desert Museum at Tucson, Arizona, is REDLIST.

Instead of people being in their own internal world and the planet, with its mountains and oceans, being 'out there,' the Earth consists of two milieus enfolding two kinds of people. The planet stockpiles its resources in myriad diverse forms such as mountains and oceans, but the number of assets marked 'miscellaneous' is so slight as to be insignificant.

As the human race moves forward with one lot called 'male' and the other called 'female,' the planet moves forward with a similar dynamic. In alternating polarity, the REDLIST array interacts with the GREENLIST array. This is the sex life of planet Earth!

ten

conclusions

Throughout this book references to lists have appeared frequently. They are divided into two orders, a REDLIST and a GREENLIST, a hitherto unsuspected polarity of environmental substances revealed by muscle-function tests with thousands of human subjects. Many with long-standing chronic complaints have felt newly able to cope with life mentally and physically since they began heeding these lists.

The lists purposely do not include brand-name products, over-the-counter medicines, prescription drugs or narcotics. That information might be valuable, even critical, but you and your family and friends must make your own tests and judgments until the day which I fantasize, when all products come pretested and clearly labeled REDLIST or GREENLIST.

The best use of these lists is as an invitation—an invitation to adopt an experimental attitude and make diet and environmental changes, little by little, to bring new health and beauty into your world. As I have said, I can only speculate as to the reason why there are opposing biotypes with such radical contrasts in bearing, demeanor—probably, ultimately, in genesis—and most notably in diet. That is the business of the universe's designer. As to how our bodies, through our subconscious minds, can instantly distinguish potentially benign or malign environmental elements, there is theoretical ground I have not trod upon.

The great, quasi-mystic psychologist and philosopher Carl Gustav Jung often dwelt upon the notion of a collective unconscious through which every thought experienced by all the human beings in history could be instantly available to our subconscious minds (analogizing us more closely to herds of zebra, schools of fish, and innumerable other communities of species—which only makes sense).

The non-local concepts of quantum mechanics, corresponding with much metaphysical supposition, make it feasible to conjecture that *all* knowledge could be subconsciously available through what the famed kinesiologist and psychiatrist David Hawkins calls a 'database of consciousness'—accounting for tarot, the *I Ching*, dowsing, telepathy, and virtually all 'psychic' phenomena as well as kinesiology.

But this is only speculation. What counts is healthy survival. Take control of your own well-being. Probably the wisest thing you could do would be to start your own small garden to provide a fresh and organic supply of foods from your list. Test the seed packets in the stores. Or test varieties at your produce market.

My friends come back from their travels bringing foreign foods, perfumes, handfuls of vegetation or gravel for me to test. Each sample invariably reveals the same secret of planet Earth—that it is an interwoven *pair* of worlds. Each of us is a citizen in one world and an alien in the other.

It is not unusual for a hypothesis to be simple and still be true. Newton had only to watch an apple fall to earth to become aware of vast forces at work. One fascinated, tenacious housewife, one patient husband, and a kitchen full of ordinary staples happened to allow focused attention to discern an emerging paradigm: we live as polarized individuals in a polarized world. When and if the large laboratories begin to research this matter, it will be exciting to see what their scientific technologies reveal—for instance, a possible DNA connection.

A book is a lonesome way to pass along a new revelation. I wish I could come with you personally. I want to see how you use it, what it means in your life, and what new information you squeeze out of it. There are so many possibilities! I am publishing laminated purse-or pocket-sized RED/GREEN lists for shopping and menu aids. Please write me with any suggestions—and tell me of your discoveries!

As we touch or tread on the earth, we experience a positive or a negative reaction in our muscle system and probably in other body systems as well. As real as the charge the earth gives us is the charge we give the earth. As we walk about the earth, we turn it on and off, probably causing our surroundings to twinkle.

And since all creatures, large and small, fall into one or the other polarity, as they wander the earth, they too turn it on and off.

A REDLIST grasshopper jumps from a RED-LIST chicory plant onto a GREENLIST plantain; REDLIST oak leaves blow against GREENLIST silver birch branches. And unaware of the whole design, REDLIST and GREENLIST men and women meet, fall in love, and bring forth REDLIST and GREENLIST children. And the planet's dance goes on.

LOVE,

Margaret Chaney

Margaret Chaney

P.O. Box 725363
Berkley, MI 48072-5363
USA

colophon

Red World/Green World was designed, edited, typeset and prepared for press on a PC publishing workstation, with master output from a LaserMaster typesetter, at **Bard Press**, 11505 E. Southern Drive, Cornville, Arizona 86325 (520-634-4075).

The book is set entirely in the Tiffany type family, with captions in Goudy Sans. The text is 12-point on a one-and-a-half pica leading. The first printing is perfect bound, on 60-lb. recycled vellum stock.

notes

REDLIST   GREENLIST